DATE DUE		

921

KEN   Elred, Patricia

     Rose Kennedy: an energizing
       spirit

Rose Kennedy
An Energizing Spirit

Rose Kennedy
An Energizing Spirit

by Patricia Mulrooney Eldred
illustrated by Harold Henriksen

Creative Education
Mankato, Minnesota 56001

Published by Creative Educational Society, Inc., 123 South Broad Street. Mankato. Minnesota 56001.
Copyright © 1975 by Creative Educational Society, Inc. International copyrights reserved in all countries.
No part of this book may be reproduced in any form without written permission from the publisher.
Printed in the United States.
Distributed by Childrens Press, 1224 West Van Buren Street, Chicago, Illinois 60607.
Library of Congress Number 75-1119   ISBN: 0-87191-423-9
Library of Congress Cataloging in Publication Data
Eldred, Patricia Mulrooney.   Rose Fitzgerald Kennedy: woman of courage.
Bibliography: p.
SUMMARY: A brief biography of the woman who throughout her life was connected with
politics as the daughter of the Mayor of Boston, the wife of the United States Ambassador
to England, and the mother of politically active sons and daughters.
1. Kennedy, Rose Fitzgerald, 1890-   —Juvenile literature.
(1. Kennedy, Rose Fitzgerald, 1890-   2. Women—Biography) I. Title.
E748.K378E42   973.9'092'4   (B) (92)   75-1119   ISBN 0-87191-423-9

INTRODUCTION

One of the highlights of Rose Fitzgerald Kennedy's long life was the election of her son, John, as 35th President of the United States in 1960. She has had many other happy moments as daughter of the Mayor of Boston, as wife of the United States Ambassador to England, and as mother of politically active sons and daughters.

She has also had many sorrowful moments. Four of her nine children have been killed. One is mentally retarded. Her husband was partially paralyzed for eight years before he died.

This book tells of Rose's gracious acceptance of both happy and sad moments. It also tells of the ways she inspired her children and others to strive for excellence and to use their talents to serve humanity.

Rose Kennedy

An Energizing Spirit

It was cold, and a sharp wind blew that Friday in January, 1961. The snow of the night before covered the streets and sidewalks and topped the monuments and government buildings with caps of white.

Such weather was unusual for Washington, D.C. But neither cold nor snow could dampen the enthusiasm of thousands of Americans who gathered to watch the inauguration of the young Irish Catholic from Boston, John Fitzgerald Kennedy, as 35th President of the United States.

Certainly no one was happier or prouder of this appealing young man than his mother, Rose Fitzgerald Kennedy.

Protecting her eyes from the glaring sun with dark glasses, and keeping warm in a mink coat, Rose listened to the new President's first speech to the country.

"And so, my fellow Americans, ask not what your country can do for you; ask what you can do for your country."

John, Rose's second son, had reached the highest office in the United States. Rose had often dreamed of seeing her children achieve greatness, and this event made her very happy.

As she listened, she recalled the words of St. Luke which she had often spoken to each of her children. "To whom much has been given, much will be required." During her long life she would have many occasions to recall these words.

The air was fresh and crisp that Friday in November, 1963. Most of the Cape Cod vacationers had left, and the noises of the summer had ceased.

Golden marigolds, black-eyed susans, and multi-colored chrysanthemums made patches of brilliant color in the large yards. Orange, yellow, and red leaves drifted slowly to the ground. It was a day to delight in the magnificence of late fall in New England.

After attending Mass at St. Francis Xavier Catholic Church, Rose Kennedy took her husband Joe for a drive around Hyannis Port so they might enjoy the splendor of the autumn day. Their children and grandchildren would be arriving in a few days to celebrate Thanksgiving. As they gazed at the scenery around them, they knew they had much to be thankful for.

But that afternoon the brilliance of the day was suddenly broken for Rose and Joe. A news report stunned not only the Kennedys but people across the country. "The President has been shot."

As they sat numb in front of radios and televisions, people slowly began to realize the awful truth. The hopes and dreams of those who had rejoiced at the inauguration in 1961 faded. President John Fitzgerald Kennedy was dead.

Certainly no one felt the loss more than Rose Fitzgerald Kennedy. Did she that day, too, recall the words, "To whom much has been given, much will be required"?

Rose Fitzgerald Kennedy has been given much during her lifetime, but she has also given much to other people. The story of her life is one of amazing strength and faith.

Rose was born and grew up in Boston. Her initiation into political life began early. Her father, John F. Fitzgerald, was elected to the United States Congress in 1894 when Rose was four. And when she graduated from the three-year program at Dorchester High School at 15, she received her diploma from her father, the newly elected mayor of Boston.

Rose apparently shared her father's determination to work hard in order to achieve high goals. She graduated in the top three in her class of 285. She completed another year at Dorchester in 1906 in order to prepare for college. Then she was accepted at Wellesley College.

Her father, however, decided she was too young for that school and sent her to the Sacred Heart Convent in Boston. She still regrets not having been able to go to the college of her choice. In 1969 she commented to a stranger at a reception in Paris, "I was accepted at Wellesley, and I wanted to go, but in those days you didn't argue with your father."

Two years later, when her father was not re-elected mayor of Boston, Rose had a chance to travel to Europe with her parents and her sister Agnes. They visited Ireland, England, Belgium, France, Switzerland, Germany, and Holland in two months. At the end of the summer the Fitzgeralds decided that Rose and Agnes should stay in Holland to attend a convent boarding school called Blumenthal.

Although Rose realized that the year was a profitable one because she could learn French and German and travel in Europe, she was eager to return home. When she and Agnes did arrive in Boston, their father was in the midst of plans for running for mayor again. This time he was elected. Shortly after this, Rose completed her formal education at Manhattanville College in New York.

Rose, as the oldest child in the family, had always been the favorite of her father. She in turn admired and respected him. But there was one subject on which they did not agree: Rose's future husband.

Rose first met Joseph Patrick Kennedy when they were both children vacationing in Maine. They met again about eight years later and began to see each other as much as they could. Rose's father did not think Joe was the right boy for his daughter and tried to get her interested in others.

But although Rose did not want to hurt her parents, she knew she loved Joe. So they continued to meet at dances, at the homes of friends, at lectures, or at the library.

After Joe graduated from Harvard, he proved he had a good understanding of the business world. He became President of the Columbia Trust Bank at the age of 25. Then Rose's father relented. Rose and Joe were married

I would rather be known as the mother of a great son or great daughter than the author of a great book or the painter of a great masterpiece

in October, 1914, in a simple ceremony, and she became Rose Fitzgerald Kennedy.

Rose's happiness at being married to Joe was equaled only by her happiness at becoming a mother in 1915 when Joe Jr. was born. She has always felt that being a mother is a very important part of her life. She once wrote a note to herself which said, "I would rather be known as the mother of a great son or great daughter than the author of a great book or the painter of a great masterpiece."

When one looks at the lives of her nine children, it is obvious that she has accomplished her goal.

John was born in 1917, followed by Rosemary, Kathleen, Eunice, Patricia, Robert, Jean, and Edward. Since Joe Sr. had become wealthy, he was able to provide large houses, housekeepers, and nurses for the children. Rose did not have the responsibility of preparing the meals, doing the wash, or changing the diapers. She spent her time helping her children form their ideas; she provided challenging and stimulating experiences for them.

From the time she was quite young, Rose found great comfort in her Catholic religion. She wanted her children to know the importance of faith, too. When they were small, she would take them walking in the morning and often stop in a church. She wanted them to begin thinking of church as a place to go any time, not just on Sunday.

Rose also thought that children should be interested in important events of the past and present. She used mealtimes to encourage discussion of such topics. She placed a bulletin board near the dining room and expected the older children to read the articles placed there. Then they would be able to contribute to the conversation at the table.

Rose tried to keep all of the children involved in these discussions. She would not permit one child to dominate the conversation. As the family grew larger, Rose felt that the difference in ages might keep the younger ones from participating.

For this reason she arranged a separate table for the younger children in another room. She would sit with them and keep the discussion on their level. If Thanksgiving were approaching, she might ask questions about the Pilgrims or the food at the first Thanksgiving. Or they might talk about a current election.

In later years when Rose saw her children taking active roles in public life, giving speeches, and participating in debates, she decided that the mealtime discussions must have been worthwhile.

Rose encouraged games which demanded mental skills. One of these games, called "Examples," she had learned from her father. She still plays it with her grandchildren who have changed the name to "Snakes." Rose might ask the children to add five and two, multiply by three, divide by seven, take away two, add eight, multiply by five, and then give the answer.

She revealed in her book, *Times to Remember,* that when Teddy (Edward Kennedy's nickname) was about ten, she went over some of the examples with him before the game with the family. When she gave these examples to the others, he shouted the answers before anyone else could. Neither she nor Teddy ever told anyone that he had had some help. The older brothers and sisters just tried harder so they wouldn't be beaten by their younger brother.

In addition to challenging her children intellectually, Rose stressed physical development. All of the children attended dancing school and took tennis and golf lessons.

The Kennedy summer house at Hyannis Port on Cape Cod had a large yard. The games of touch football played there have become famous. There would be lots of shouting and running and serious playing. Everyone, regardless of age, got into the game.

After a weekend of trying to keep up with the active Kennedys, one visitor wrote a set of "Rules for Visiting the Kennedys." He mentioned the football games. "It's 'touch' but it's murder. If you don't want to play, don't come. If you do come, play; or you'll be fed in the kitchen and nobody will speak to you. Don't let the girls fool you. Even pregnant, they can make you look silly."

The Kennedy parents strongly believed in doing one's best at everything. Joe used to say, "We don't want any losers around here. In this family we want winners."

Some people have criticized this strong competitive spirit, but Rose has defended it. She says that she and her husband were not interested in winning in itself, but were trying to teach the children to put all their effort into anything they did — work or play or study. They wanted each child to develop all his talents.

Although the children did compete against one another in sailing, football, tennis, and most sports, they also shared a special feeling of family loyalty. They called their sailboat the Tenovous. After Teddy was born and the name no longer applied, they bought a new boat which they named Onemore.

Rose and Joe encouraged the children to work and play with each other. Once, when Joe Jr. and his father were debating about the economy, Jack (as they called John) told his mother that he liked his brother's ideas better than his father's. When Joe Sr. heard this, he told Rose, "I don't care what the boys think about my ideas. I can always look out for myself. The important thing is that they should stick together."

Rose's own love of travel probably made her realize its value for her children. When Kathleen was 16, Rose took her to Russia. In 1936 it was unusual for two women to travel so far alone. Even Kathleen asked why they were going. "Because it's interesting," was her mother's reply. Rose tried to make sure that each of the children had an opportunity to travel and study in Europe.

Since foreign countries intrigued Rose, she was especial-

ly pleased when Joe Sr. was appointed Ambassador to England by President Franklin Roosevelt in 1938. He and his family would live in that country while he held the position.

The English people were fascinated by the lively Kennedy family. The people especially commented on Rose's youthful appearance. They found it hard to tell who was the mother in the photos of the family.

The Ambassador's house in London was called the Embassy. It had 36 rooms. Rose had 23 servants and three chauffeurs. As representatives of the United States Government, Rose and Joe entertained many important people at the Embassy. On one occasion they even had the King and Queen of England as guests for dinner.

The activity and excitement of this type of life appealed to Rose. She loved meeting new people and sharing ideas and experiences with them.

When World War II broke out in 1939, Rose and the children returned to the United States because the situation in England could have been dangerous for them. Then in November of 1940 Joe offered his resignation as Ambassador because he disagreed with President Roosevelt's foreign policy.

About this time Rose and Joe found themselves facing a difficult decision. They had known for a long time that their oldest daughter, Rosemary, was not as capable as the other children. She would try to play tennis or football as the others did, but she was not well co-ordinated. When

she was old enough to learn to read and write, she had problems.

When they noticed Rosemary's trouble, Rose and Joe took her to doctors. They learned that she was mentally retarded. The doctors suggested that Rose and Joe put Rosemary in a special home. But they refused to do this. They thought they could do more for their daughter if they kept her with the family. They didn't want her to miss the fun that the other children had.

For years Joe and Rose said almost nothing about Rosemary's condition. They didn't even tell the other children that there was something seriously wrong. They tried to treat Rosemary the same way they treated the other children, but they always made sure that someone was looking after her.

As Rosemary grew older, she often became frustrated. She couldn't go out in a rowboat or to the train station alone as the others did, and she couldn't understand why.

It was extremely difficult for Rose to watch her pretty daughter having these problems. She wanted to give Rosemary as much joy as she could. She spent a great deal of time helping her and keeping her involved in activities. She arranged a trip to Switzerland for Rosemary and Eunice when they were both teenagers. Rosemary made her social debut in England at the same time her younger sister Kathleen did. And Rosemary attended a school in England where she made some progress.

Finally, however, in 1941, Rose and Joe realized that

Rosemary had reached a stage where she needed more help than they could give her. They agreed that she would be better off in a special school. They selected St. Coletta's in Jefferson, Wisconsin. The nuns there were able to give Rosemary the special attention she needed.

This decision caused Rose much pain, but her faith in God helped her cope with the situation. She felt God must have a reason for her daughter's illness, and so she tried to accept it as part of His plan. Rose has visited Rosemary every few months since 1941. The other Kennedys also try to see her regularly.

Not long after this decision was reached, Rose and Joe began to be concerned about Kathleen, too. She had fallen in love with William John Robert Cavendish, the Marquess of Hartington, a young man she first met when her father was Ambassador to England.

The main problem about the relationship concerned

religion. Kathleen was Roman Catholic, and Billy belonged to the Church of England. Each of them had been brought up to believe very firmly in his religion, and neither could change his beliefs.

The Kennedys and the Cavendishes tried everything to get special permission for the two to marry with the blessing of both churches. However, nothing could be done.

Finally, in May, 1944, Kathleen and Billy decided to be married even though they could not have a church ceremony. This was hard for Rose since her religion meant so much to her. It was disappointing to have her daughter marry outside the Catholic Church. She did not attend Kathleen's wedding in England. Only Joe Jr. was there to represent the Kennedy family.

By this time, with America deeply involved in World War II, both Joe Jr. and Jack had joined the Navy. Joe had volunteered for training as a Navy flyer, and in 1943

he was sent to England to fly B-24's with the British Coastal Command. Jack was serving on PT boats in the South Pacific.

Rose, like most mothers, worried about her sons. And the war did bring tragedies to the Kennedys.

On a Sunday afternoon in 1944, after a picnic lunch outdoors, Rose answered a knock on the door. She found two Catholic priests there who wished to speak to her and her husband. They explained quietly that Joe Jr. had been killed while flying on a special mission.

It was hard news to accept. Joe, the oldest of the children, had been intelligent, courageous, enthusiastic. He had dreamed of being President, and only a few years earlier he had begun making a name for himself on the political scene. It seemed impossible to Rose and Joe Sr. that he was dead. Some people say that Joe Sr. was never the same after that. When people wanted to talk about his son, he would tell them to speak to Rose. He couldn't talk of him.

Rose may have been able to talk about Joe, but in her book about the Kennedy family, she wrote, "It has been said that time heals all wounds. I don't agree. The wounds remain. Time — the mind protecting its sanity — covers them with some scar tissue and the pain lessens, but it is never gone."

Before the family could recover from the shock of Joe's death, they learned that Billy, Kathleen's husband of six months, had also been killed in action.

Since she loved her children so much, the loss of a son

and a son-in-law was heartbreaking. But Rose knew that she had to face reality and continue to be a support for the rest of the family. Many years later she wrote about her ability to rise above even the greatest tragedy. "Birds sing after a storm; why shouldn't people feel as free to delight in whatever sunlight remains to them?"

It wasn't long, then, before she was involved in something which had always appealed to her: political campaigning. After the war, Jack decided to run for representative to the United States Congress. He campaigned in the same district that his grandfather, John Fitzgerald, had represented 52 years earlier.

Rose was not just a figurehead in the campaign. Dave Powers, who was one of Jack's main advisors and later became a special assistant to the President, said, "In 1946, she had a greater understanding of precinct politics than anyone in our organization . . . She not only loved meeting people, but she cared about the people she met."

Rose knew the district, and people knew her because of her appearances with her father years before. She also knew the important aspects of precinct politics. Dave Powers recalls that she was horrified at one rally when she found that nobody was getting the names of those who attended so that later contacts could be made.

With his mother's help and that of his brothers and sisters who also worked for him, Jack won the primary and the election. At 29 he entered the Congress of the United States.

It was only two years later when tragedy shook their lives again. Kathleen had been living in England since her husband's death. In 1948 she was flying in a small private plane in southern France. Bad weather and inadequate navigation equipment caused the plane to crash into a mountain. All on board were killed.

This death, too, affected Rose deeply. Kathleen was only 28 when she was killed. She had been generous and active. Since the war she had been working in England to help the country recover. Again Rose demonstrated her strength. She was able to accept the sorrow and carry on. Years later in an interview, she said she felt it was important "not to think of what might have been, but to devote your time, efforts, and energies to the living, and to the immediate challenges. In this way we turn our heartaches into constructive efforts to lighten the sorrows of others."

Fortunately, Jack's public life kept Rose busy. He was re-elected to Congress in 1948, and in 1952 he ran against Henry Cabot Lodge for a seat in the United States Senate. Lodge had been the Senator from Massachusetts since 1936 and had a strong hold on the position. But the Kennedy campaigners went to work. And, as always, they worked hard. Rose again did her share of public speaking. She prepared well for her appearances. She would find out what type of people she would be speaking to and adapt her talks to their needs and interests.

Dave Powers remembers that every night for six weeks he would pick Rose up in the evening, and they would go from meeting to meeting. Rose would often change clothes in the car so she would be dressed appropriately for the gathering. All of the time and work proved fruitful, for Jack defeated Lodge and took his seat in the Senate.

During his years in the Senate Jack became better known to people across the country. During the late 50's he began his drive for his next goal: the Presidency.

Jack was selected as the Democratic candidate for President in 1960. Rose was nearly 70, but she was in the forefront of the campaign this time, too. Always conscious of her appearance, she was especially concerned with how she looked in this race because of the use of television. To stay trim she took daily walks, played golf often, and swam frequently in the cold water of Hyannis Port. She also took yearly trips to Paris to buy clothes, so she was always in style.

Again the Kennedy teamwork was successful. John Fitzgerald Kennedy became President, and Rose was mother of the President of the United States.

The inauguration was a triumph. Rose was proud of her son. He was doing what she thought was most important: using his abilities to serve others.

The two and a half years her son was President were happy ones. Rose visited the White House often. She attended some formal state dinners, and she greatly enjoyed being with her grandchildren Caroline and John.

She also had an opportunity to accompany the President and his wife Jackie on some of their travels. She was in Paris with them to meet the President of France, Charles de Gaulle. She was also in Vienna when the President met Russian Premier Nikita Khrushchev.

But in the midst of this happiness, another crisis occurred. In December of 1961, Joe had a stroke. Partially paralyzed, he lost his power of speech. Rose ached for her husband who had been so energetic. She knew the frustration he experienced as he tried diligently to recover his strength. She spent much time with him, doing all she could to encourage him and to make him comfortable.

Joe's stroke was a blow to the whole family. The children

had depended on their father's advice and encouragement. He had been extremely helpful to the boys in their careers. Perhaps Rose realized that Joe's stroke only increased her responsibility for the family.

There was still more work to be done. Ted's turn at a political career had come. In 1962 he ran for the United States Senate. Ted won the election. At this time Rose had three sons in important positions in the government. Jack was President, Bobby was Attorney General of the United States, and Ted was a Senator.

In her book, Rose calls the days that followed a "golden time." There were the summers at Hyannis Port with her children and grandchildren visiting, the football games on the lawn, and the joyous Christmas holidays at Palm Beach, Florida. Even though Joe was an invalid, he could enjoy the family gatherings. And the Kennedys found great happiness in being together.

But the golden days did not last for long. At their peak, Jack was shot and killed in Dallas. For hours after she heard the news on that Friday in November, Rose walked the beach at Hyannis Port praying and wondering, "Why Jack?" He had so much to give his family, his friends, and his country. He was young and full of ideas and enthusiasm for the future.

The tragedy affected the whole country. People watched the Kennedy family during those grief-filled days of the

death and funeral. They saw sorrow, but they also saw strength.

Even with this pain, Rose continued the work of the living.

The next work was helping Bobby become Senator from New York. Rose entered that campaign, too, and Bobby was victorious.

Then Bobby decided to try for the Democratic presidential nomination in 1968. Rose at 77 was there again, shaking hands, giving speeches, telling Bobby he should have his hair cut, and should talk slower.

Campaigning was more tiring this time, but Rose still enjoyed it. In June, 1968, after campaigning in the western states and in California, she flew to Hyannis Port. There, on June 4, she watched the results of the California primary on television. By eleven that night it seemed as though Bobby had enough of a lead for a victory, and Rose went to bed, perhaps to dream of another son as President.

The nightmare began the next morning. For as she dressed for Mass, it was not news of Bobby's victory that she heard. The news was that Bobby had been shot and was in serious condition. He died the following day.

As she did after Jack's death, Rose prayed and wondered why another tragedy should strike her family. There was no sense to the violence. She knew that Bobby was, as Teddy said at the funeral Mass, ". . . a good and decent man, who saw wrong and tried to right it, saw suffering and tried to

heal it, saw war and tried to stop it."

Rose summarized her deep feelings about Bobby in her book. She wrote, "I know that I shall not look on his like again."

After all of these tragic events, a lesser woman might have weakened. And everyone would have understood. But Rose, with her incredible courage and poise and ability to weather tragedy, appeared on national television after the funeral to express her thanks to those who had extended sympathy to the family.

". . . We accept with faith and resignation His Holy Will, with no looking back to what might have been, and we are at peace. We have courage, we are undaunted and steadfast, and we shall carry on the principles for which Bobby stood . . ."

After Bobby's death, Joe's health declined, and in November of 1969 he died. For 54 years Rose and Joe had worked together to support and encourage each other and their children. His death left an emptiness in Rose's life that could never be filled.

But even this death she was able to handle with dignity. At the funeral Mass Ted read a prayer written by his mother. "I thank Thee, O my God, with all my heart for all Thou has done for me. I thank Thee, especially, for my husband, who with your help has made possible so many joys and such great happiness in my life."

Again Rose continued to find comfort and purpose in

remaining active. She continued to work for the Joseph P. Kennedy Foundation which Joe Sr. had established after Joe Jr.'s death as a memorial to his son. The foundation benefits the mentally retarded.

She continued to travel. In 1970 she flew to Switzerland to a health resort for a short stay, then to Greece to visit Jackie and Aristotle Onassis, and then to Ethiopia to celebrate her 80th birthday with Emperor Haile Selassie whose birthday is close to her own.

She continued to walk three or four miles a day and to swim in the sea every morning she could. She did, however, on her 84th birthday, in 1974, say that she would be giving up golf.

She continued to correspond with her grandchildren. When she entertains or visits them, she talks about the same ideas she stressed with her children. She is interested in their mental alertness, intellectual curiosity, physical fitness, and service to others.

Her grandchildren respond to her with the same admiration her children have always given her. Chris Lawford, Patricia's son, once wrote that he thought his grandmother's goal in influencing her children and grandchildren "has been to try to teach them to teach themselves."

Rose Fitzgerald Kennedy, the woman who has given direction to so many lives, continues to live a life which reflects her understanding of St. Luke's words: "To whom much has been given, much will be required."

Patricia Mulrooney Eldred

Pat was born in Manistique, Michigan, but spent most of her childhood and teenage years in St. Paul, Minnesota.

She began her writing career at about age nine and kept her manuscripts carefully protected in a folder labeled "My Story-ies."

In 1964 she received a BA degree from Mundelein College, Chicago.

She spent nine years teaching high school English and journalism — first in a small school in Iowa City, Iowa, and later in a large public school in a Chicago suburb. She was also advisor to high school newspaper staffs for six years.

In the spring of 1974 she and her husband Ron and daughter Sheila moved back to St. Paul where they plan to make their home.

Harold Henriksen

Harold was born in St. Paul, Minnesota and has lived there most of his life. He attended the School of the Associated Arts in St. Paul.

Even while serving in the Army, Harold continued to keep alive his desire to become an artist. In 1965 he was a winner in the All Army Art Contest.

After the Army, Harold returned to Minnesota where he worked for several art studios in the Minneapolis-St. Paul area. In 1967 he became an illustrator for one of the largest art studios in Minneapolis.

During 1971 Harold and his wife traveled to South America where he did on-the-spot drawings for a year. Harold, his wife and daughter Maria now live in Minneapolis where he works as a free lance illustrator.

close ups

Walt Disney

Bob Hope

Duke Ellington

Dwight Eisenhower

Coretta King

Pablo Picasso

Ralph Nader

Bill Cosby

Dag Hammarskjold

Sir Frederick Banting

Mark Twain

Beatrix Potter

Margaret Mead

Rose Kennedy

Walter Cronkite

Henry Kissinger